CHINESE BRAIN TWISTERS

CHINESE BRAIN TWISTERS

Fast, Fun Puzzles That Help Children Develop Quick Minds

BAIFANG

John Wiley & Sons, Inc.
New York   Chichester   Brisbane   Toronto   Singapore

Library of Congress Cataloging-in-Publication Data:

Baifang
   Chinese brain twisters: fast, fun puzzles that help children develop quick
   minds/compiled by Baifang.
      p. cm.
   ISBN 0-471-59505-5 (alk. paper)
    1. Puzzles. 2. Amusements–China. I. Title.
GV1493.B212 1993
793.73–dc20   93-10862

Printed in the United States of America

10 9 8 7 6 5 4 3 2

Contents

Introduction

There is wisdom in the old Chinese saying "Things learned during childhood remain with one forever." When I was growing up in the north of China during the 1950s and 1960s, my family and friends taught me many of the puzzles included in this book. My parents recalled others from their childhood in the 1930s and 1940s.

Such puzzles are part of China's folk culture. They have endured for centuries, even through the Communist era of Mao Zedong, when so many other traditional ways of life were lost. They speak of the commitment of most Chinese parents to expand their children's intellectual capacities during even their earliest years.

Hoping to bring this tradition to my adopted country, I collected some of the best puzzles to put in this small book. I hope you and your children enjoy them as much as I have.

Baifang

Instructions

The book is divided into three parts: Sticks and Shapes, Sticks and Numbers, and Words and Numbers. Each contains puzzles that help develop agile, creative minds. These mental calisthenics will also help prepare your child for a lifetime of clear, logical thinking. Playing with real sticks allows your child to manipulate the concepts and leads to even greater learning.

Who can solve these puzzles?

Anyone above the age of eight can enjoy the puzzles. When I was a child, my family introduced me to the easiest ones first. As I learned how to solve them, I tried to remember the solutions so that I could solve them faster the next time I saw them.

Although your child may work his or her way through the book alone, it is much more fun to share the experience. You can do these puzzles together at any place, at almost any time—at home, on vacation, on a plane or train, or even while camping. One person can work on them alone, of course, or a group can turn them into a game by competing against each other or against the clock.

What do you need to solve the puzzles?

You'll need a pen or pencil, some paper, and a flat surface. You'll also need about 50 short sticks. Toothpicks or matchsticks are just the right length. You can also use straws cut into equal lengths, about two inches long.

To solve the puzzles, form the patterns with your sticks or draw them on a piece of paper.

Rules for the puzzles:

To **move** sticks means to shift the position of a stick without reducing the original number.

To **remove** a given number of sticks means to take away, thus reducing the number of sticks in the pattern.

To **add** means to increase a given number of sticks.

Let's try one stick puzzle together:

These **three** diamonds can be changed into **four** equilateral (equal-sided) triangles by moving **two** sticks. Which **two** should be moved?

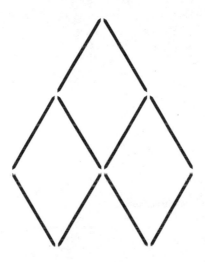

Turn the page to find the solution.

Start

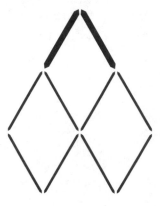

Here the thick lines show
the sticks to be moved.

Finish

And here the thick lines
show the new position
of the moved sticks.

Now let's begin!

Sticks and Shapes

By moving only **two** sticks, these **three** equal-sized squares can be changed into **four** equal-sized rectangles. Which **two** sticks should be moved?

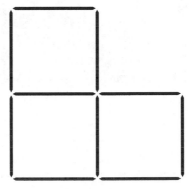

Start

Finish

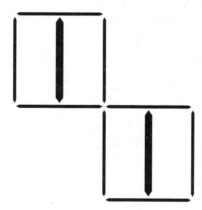

This Y-like figure can be turned upside down by moving **two** sticks. Which **two** should be moved?

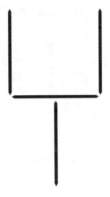

Start

Finish

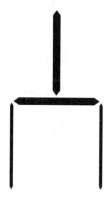

This shovel is made of four sticks. How can these four sticks be made into a chair? How can they be made into a stool?

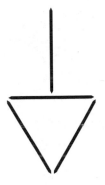

Start

Finish

Finish

CHAIR

STOOL

This pattern can be changed into **one** diamond and **one** equilateral (equal-sided) triangle by moving **two** sticks. Which **two** should be moved?

Start

Finish

By moving only **two** sticks, the gap at the bottom left corner of this pattern can be closed up, leaving **two** squares. Which **two** sticks should be moved?

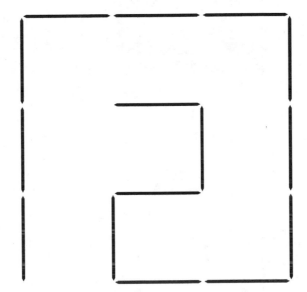

Start

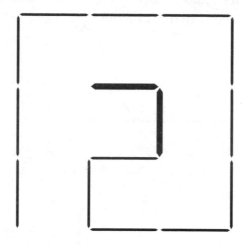

Finish

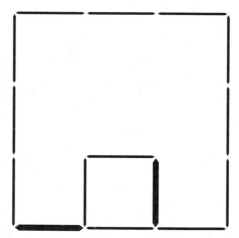

This house can be changed into **two** houses by moving only **one** stick. Which **one** should be moved?

Start

Finish

This pattern is made of **three** equal-sized rectangles. How can it be changed into **six** squares by moving only **three** sticks?

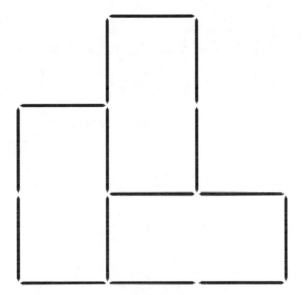

Start

Finish

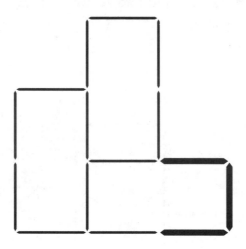

These two rectangles can be changed into **two** squares by moving **two** sticks. Which **two** should be moved?

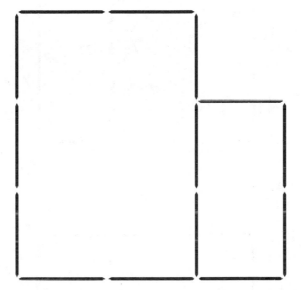

Start

Finish

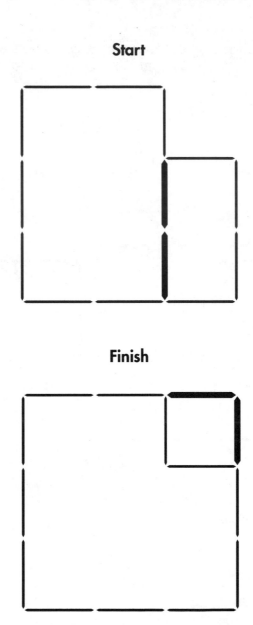

How can this pattern be changed into **three** squares by moving only **three** sticks?

(There is more than one solution.)

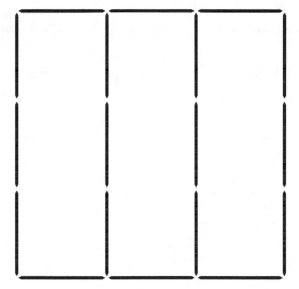

SOLUTION A

Start

Finish

SOLUTION B

Start

Finish

How can this dog be made to turn around by moving
only **one** stick?

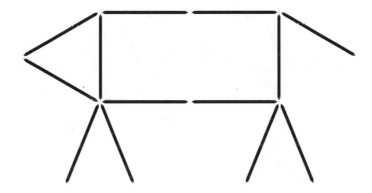

Start

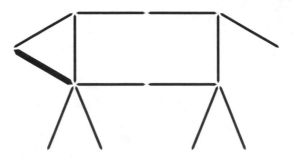

Finish

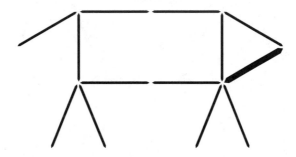

How can this dog be made to look back by moving only **two** sticks?

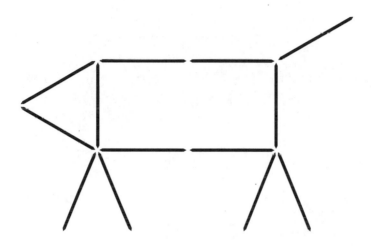

Start

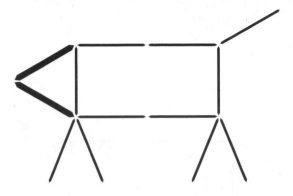

Finish

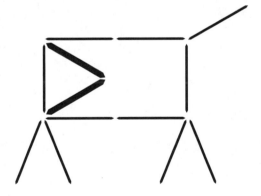

This pattern can be changed into a cube (three-dimensional square) by moving **three** sticks. Which **three** should be moved?

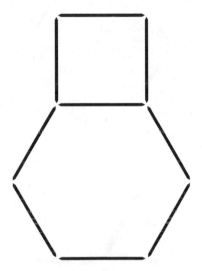

Start

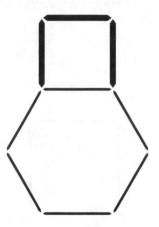

Finish

This L-shaped pattern can be changed into **four** equal-sized squares by moving **four** sticks. Which **four** sticks should be moved?

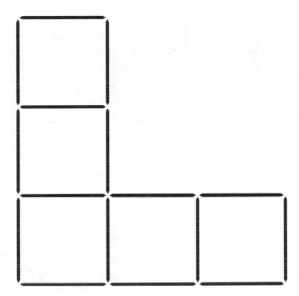

Start

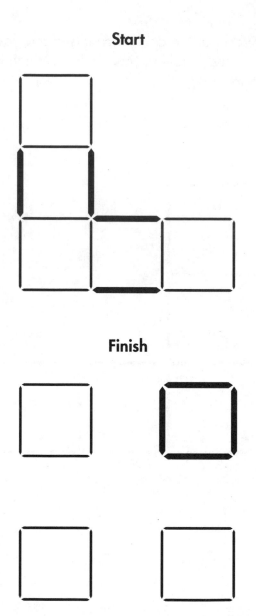

Finish

This L-shaped pattern can be changed into **four** equal-sized squares by moving only **two** sticks. Which **two** should be moved?

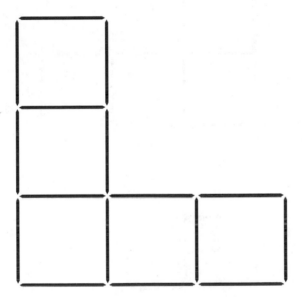

Start

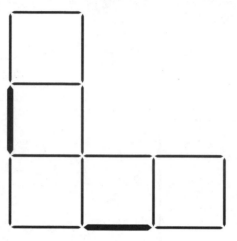

Finish

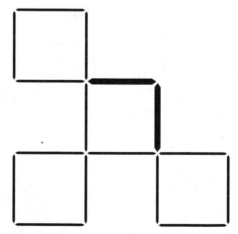

This L-shaped pattern can be changed into **three** squares by moving **four** sticks. Which **four** should be moved?

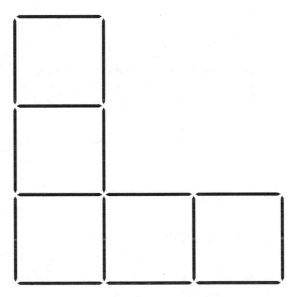

Start

Finish

This L-shaped pattern can be changed into **two** squares by moving **six** sticks. Which **six** should be moved?

(There is more than one solution.)

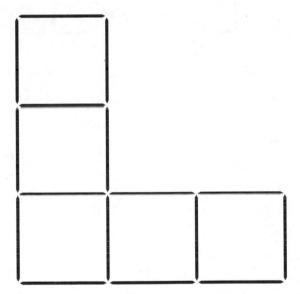

SOLUTION A

Start

Finish

SOLUTION B

Start

Finish

This pattern can be turned **upside down** by moving **four** sticks. Which **four** should be moved?

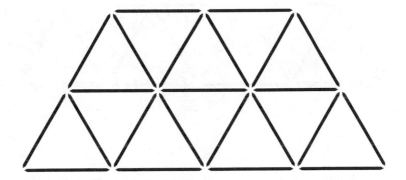

Start

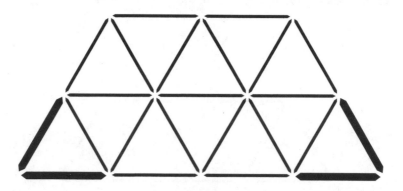

Finish

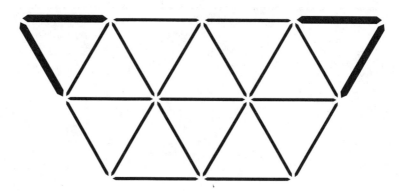

This equilateral (equal-sided) triangle can be changed into **five** equilateral triangles by moving **five** sticks. Which **five** should be moved?

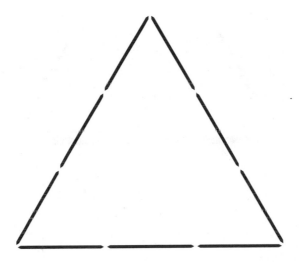

Start

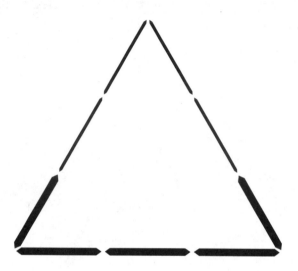

Finish

This pattern can be changed into **six** equilateral (equal-sided) triangles by removing **three** sticks. Which **three** should be removed?

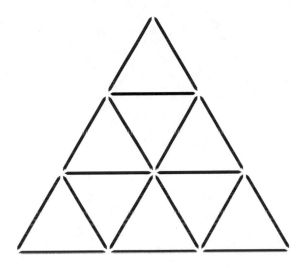

Start

Finish

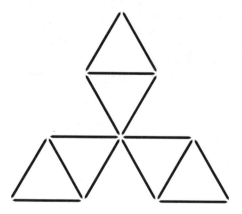

This pattern can be changed into **five** equilateral (equal-sided) trianges by removing **four** sticks. Which **four** should be removed?

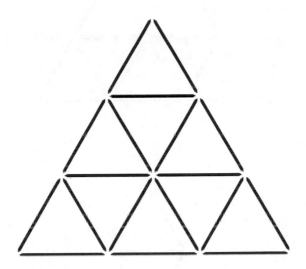

Start

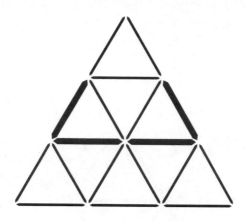

Finish

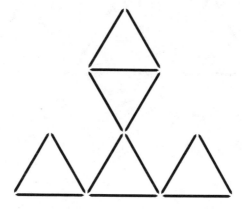

1. This pattern is made of **six** equal-sized equilateral (equal-sided) triangles. By moving **two** sticks, it can be changed into **five** equal-sized equilateral triangles. Which **two** should be moved?

2. The resulting pattern of **five** equilateral triangles can be changed into **four** equilateral triangles by moving **two** sticks. Which **two** should be moved?

3. The resulting pattern of **four** equilateral triangles can be changed into **three** equilateral triangles by moving **two** sticks. Which **two** should be moved?

4. Finally, the pattern of **three** equilateral triangles can be changed into **two** equilateral triangles by moving **two** sticks. Which **two** should be moved?

Start   **Finish**

1

2

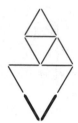

3

4

This pattern is made of **five** squares. By moving **eight** sticks, it can be changed into **nine** squares. Which **eight** should be moved?

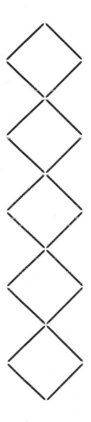

Start　　　　　　　**Finish**

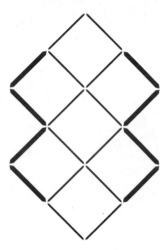

By moving **three** sticks, you can make this goldfish turn around and swim in the **opposite direction**. Which **three** should be moved?

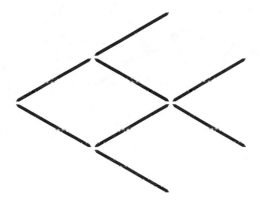

Start

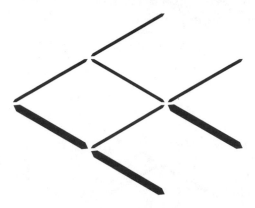

Finish

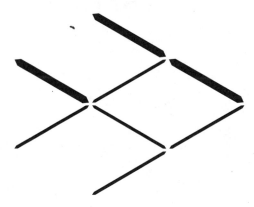

How can this pattern be changed into **five** equal-sized squares by removing **four** sticks?

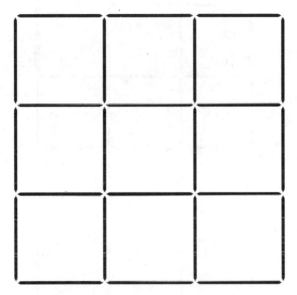

Start

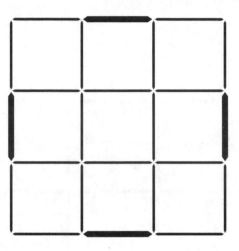

Finish

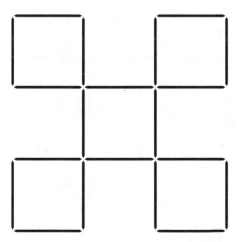

How can this pattern be changed into **three** squares by removing **six** sticks?

(There is more than one solution.)

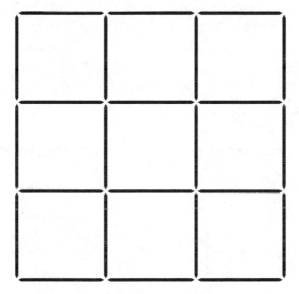

SOLUTION A

Start

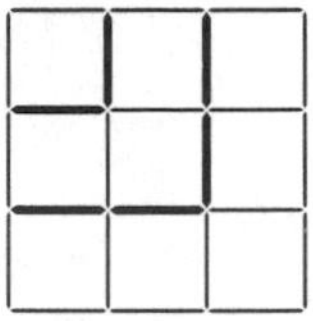

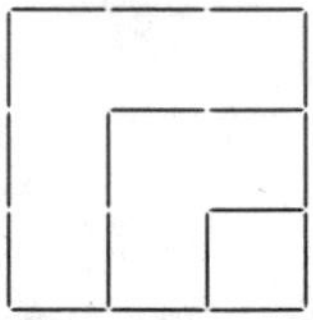

SOLUTION B

Start

Finish

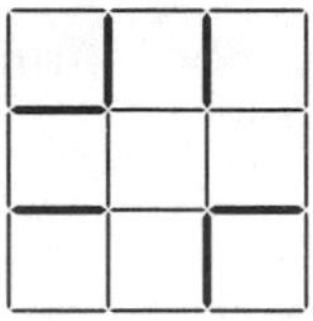

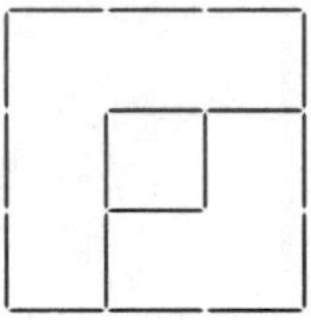

Finish

SOLUTION C

Start

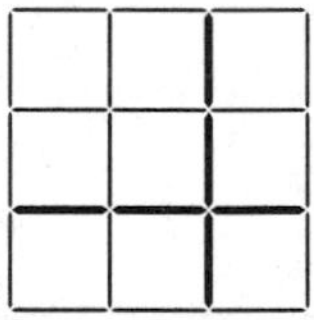

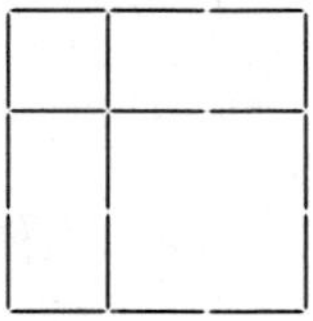

SOLUTION D

Start

Finish

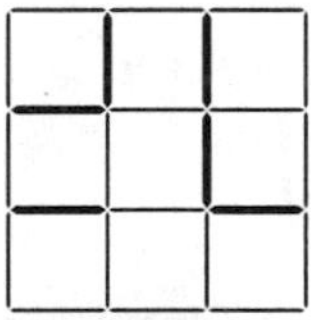

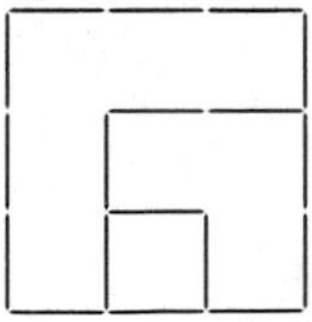

Finish

How can this pattern be changed into **two** squares by removing **eight** sticks?

(There is more than one solution.)

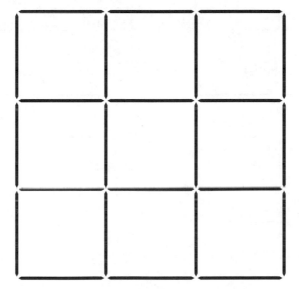

SOLUTION A

Start

Finish

SOLUTION B

Start

Finish

The number of triangles in this pattern can be reduced to **four** by removing **four** sticks. Which **four** should be removed?

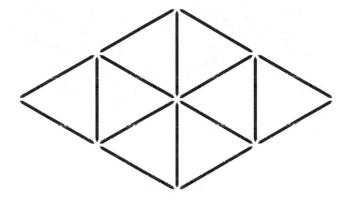

Start

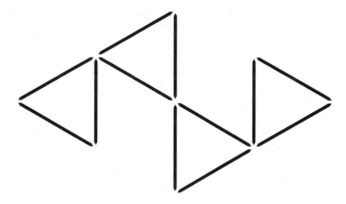

Finish

This table lamp can be changed into **five** triangles by moving **three** sticks. Which **three** should be moved?

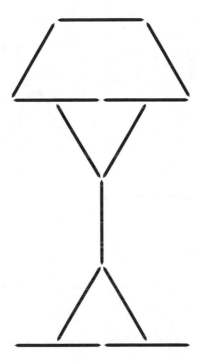

Start

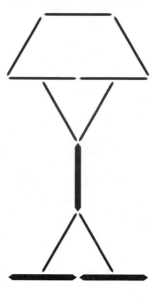

Finish

How can this pattern be changed into **six** diamonds by moving **four** sticks?

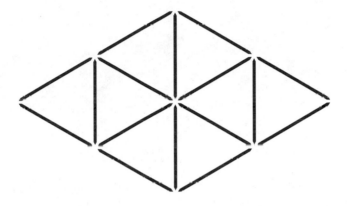

Start

Finish

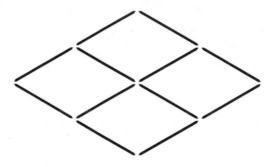

This key can be changed into **three** equal-sized squares by moving **four** sticks. Which **four** should be moved?

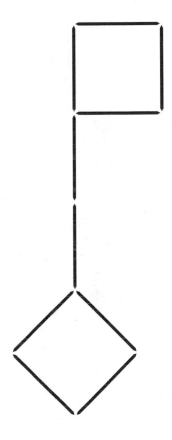

Start

Finish

This pattern can be changed into **nine** squares by moving **four** sticks. Which **four** should be moved?

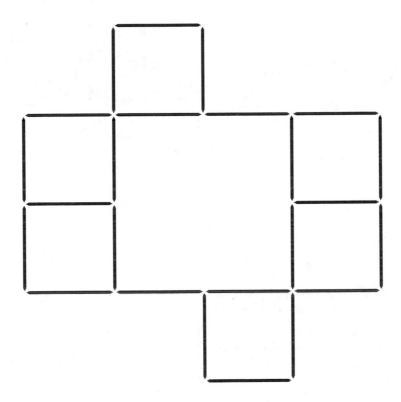

Start

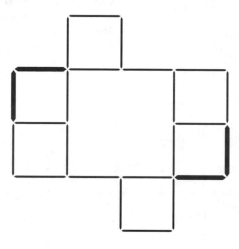

Finish

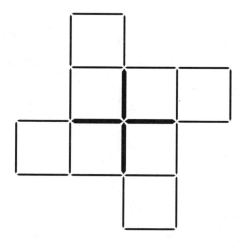

How can this pattern be divided into **four** identical shapes by adding **five** sticks?

Start

Finish

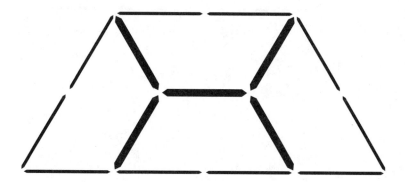

This pattern can be divided into **four** quarters by adding **eight** sticks. Where should the **eight** sticks go?

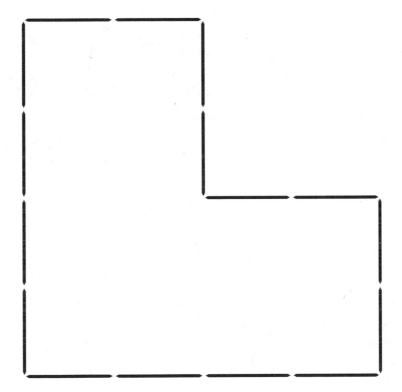

Start

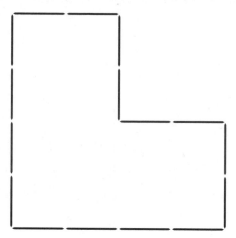

Finish

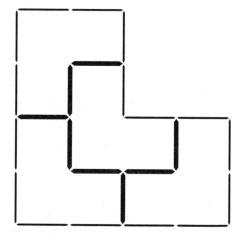

This pattern can be changed into **six** diamonds by moving **six** sticks. Which **six** should be moved?

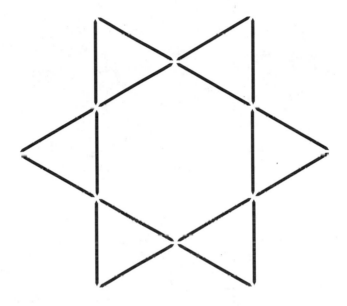

Start

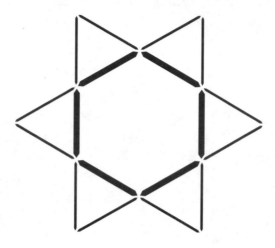

Finish

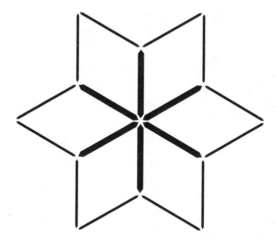

This equilateral (equal-sided) triangle can be divided into **three** identical shapes by adding **three** sticks. Where should the **three** sticks go?

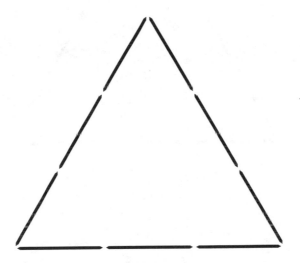

Start

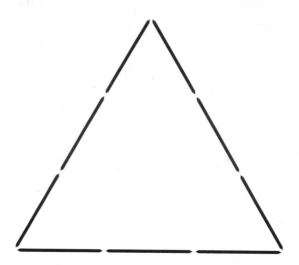

Finish

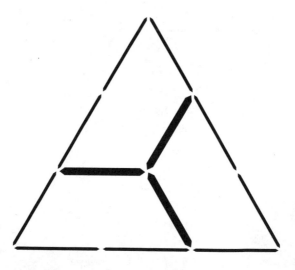

This pattern can be changed into **two** equal-sized triangles by moving **four** sticks. Which **four** should be moved?

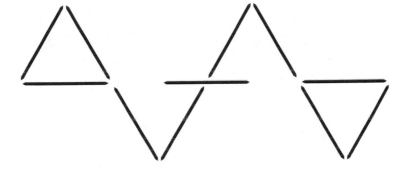

Start

Finish

This Christmas tree can be changed into a goldfish by moving **two** sticks. Which **two** should be moved?

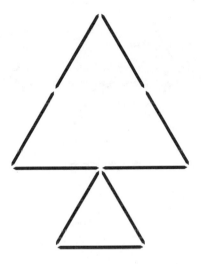

Start

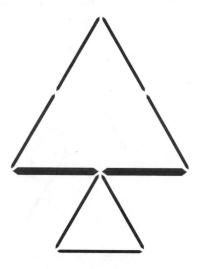

Finish

By moving **four** sticks, these **five** equal-sized squares can be reduced to **three** squares. Which **four** sticks should be moved?

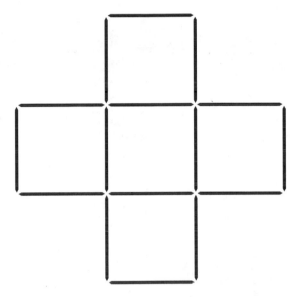

Start

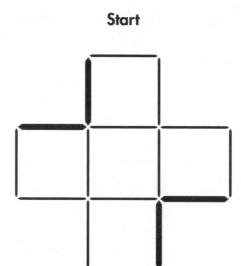

Finish

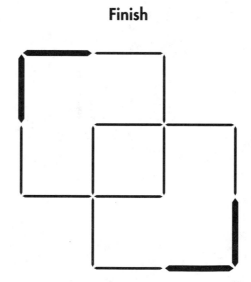

By adding **eight** sticks, this pattern can be divided into **three** identical shapes. Where should the **eight** sticks go?

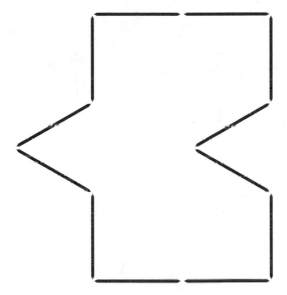

Start

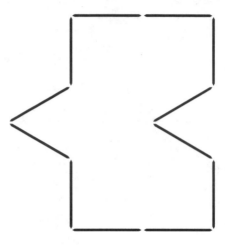

Finish

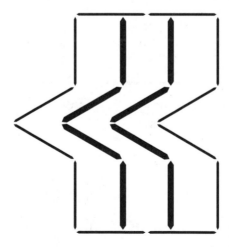

This pattern is made up of many squares. By removing **nine** sticks, it can be transformed into a pattern that will have **no squares** but **all rectangles**. Which **nine** should be removed?

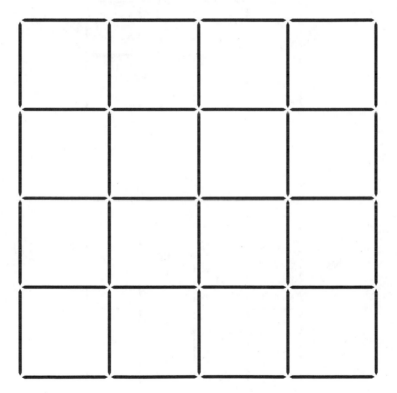

Start

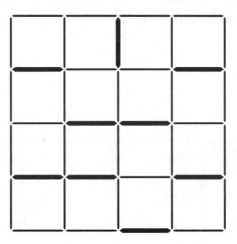

Finish

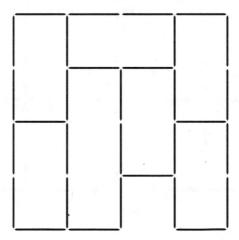

This pattern is made up of many squares. By removing **eight** sticks, it can be changed into **two** squares and **eight** equal-sized rectangles. Which **eight** should be removed?

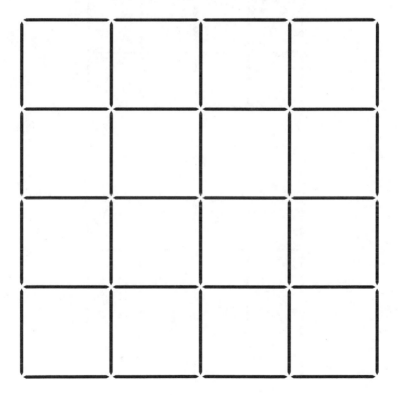

Start

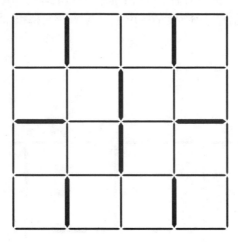

Finish

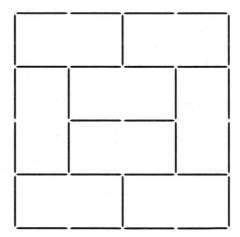

By removing **six** sticks, **half** of the equal-sized squares can be eliminated. Which **six** should be removed?

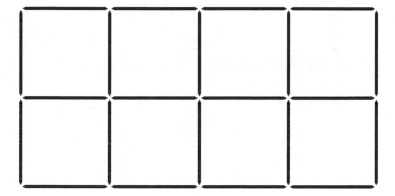

Start

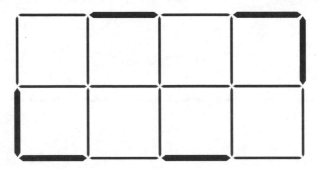

Finish

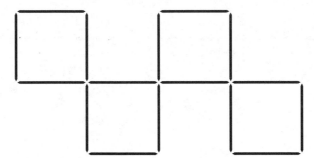

Sticks and Numbers

This math problem is incorrect, but moving only **one** stick will make it correct. Which **one** should be moved?

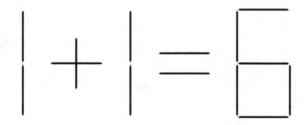

Start

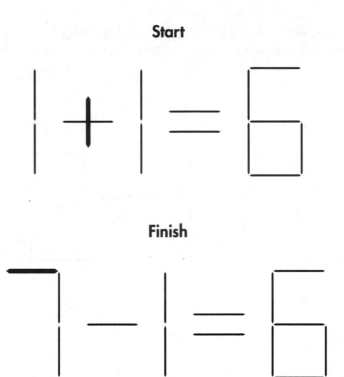

Finish

This math problem is incorrect, but moving **one** stick will make it correct. Which **one** should be moved?

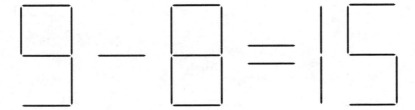

Start

$$9 - 8 = 15$$

Finish

$$9 + 6 = 15$$

This math problem is incorrect, but moving **one** stick will make it correct. Which **one** should be moved?

Start

$$99 - 59 = 10$$

Finish

$$69 - 59 = 10$$

This math problem is incorrect, but moving **two** sticks will make it correct. Which **two** should be moved?

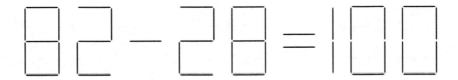

Start

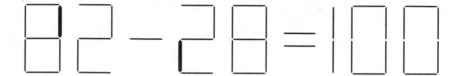

Finish

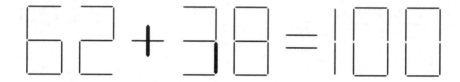

This Roman-numeral math problem is incorrect, but moving **one** stick will make it correct. Which **one** should be moved?

Start

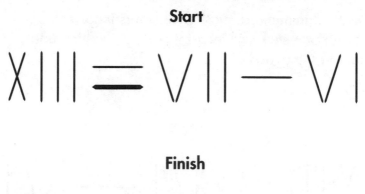

Finish

This Roman-numeral math problem is incorrect, but moving **one** stick will make it correct. Which **one** should be moved?

Start

Finish

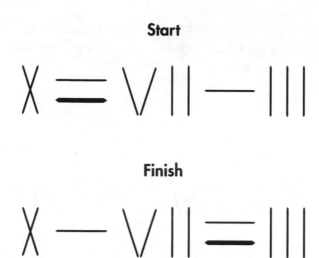

This Roman-numeral math problem is incorrect, but moving **one** stick will make it correct. Which **one** should be moved?

Start

$$XI + V = V$$

Finish

$$XI - V = VI$$

Words and Numbers

A long, long time ago in a small village in the north of China, the peasants knew that in the village pond there were two types of creatures—frogs and *chans*. The peasants were able to count a total of **3,600** creatures with a total of **13,000** legs in their pond.

Can you figure out how many frogs and how many *chans* there were in the pond?

(A *chan* is a three-legged froglike mythical creature, which was believed to bring good fortune).

Start

If all the **3,600** creatures in the pond were frogs, there would have been a total of **14,400** legs, which is **1,400** legs more than the peasants counted. Since we know that a *chan* has only three rather than four legs, we can arrive at the correct answer by the following computation.

Finish

First, if there were only frogs, then

3,600 creatures x 4 legs = 14,400 legs

But the leg count is 13,000.

14,400 legs – 13,000 legs = 1,400 legs
in the pond

If, for instance, there were 1,400 *chans*, and the remaining creatures were frogs, then

3,600 creatures – 1,400 *chans* = 2,200 frogs

Therefore:

1,400 *chans* x 3 legs = 4,200 legs
2,200 *chans* x 4 legs = 8,800 legs
13,000 legs

Thus, the pond contained **1,400** *chans* and **2,200** frogs.

A long time ago in China, there was a temple on the side of a big mountain. In the temple there were **100** old monks and young monks. Nobody knew the exact number of those who were young and those who were old. What was known was that altogether the monks ate **100** steamed buns for lunch each day, with each old monk eating **3** steamed buns while every **3** young monks shared **1** steamed bun.

Can you figure out the precise number of old and young monks in the temple?

Start

If there were only old monks in the temple, then they would have needed **300** steamed buns. However, since there were only **100** steamed buns, we can safely assume that there must have been more young monks than old monks because young monks ate less than the old monks. From what the problem tells us, we can also assume that the number of young monks has to be divisible by **3**.

Finish

First, let's try a few numbers for young monks that are divisible by 3.

If, for instance, there were 60 young monks, they would have eaten 20 steamed buns, leaving 40 old monks to eat 120 buns.

But there were only 100 steamed buns to go around.

Let's try again. If there were 66 young monks, the remaining 34 old monks alone would have eaten 102 steamed buns, so this we know would not be correct either. But if we start with 75 young monks, who would eat 25 steamed buns, that leaves 75 steamed buns, which divides by 3 perfectly into 25.

Thus, the temple contained **75** young monks and **25** old monks.

There were two peasant families living in the Ming Dynasty who had one urn between them filled with **10** *jin* of cooking oil. They also had two ladles, one of which could hold **7** *jin* of oil, while the other could hold only **3** *jin*.

Using only these containers, how could these two families equally divide their **10** *jin* of cooking oil?

(A *jin* is a Chinese measurement.)

Start

The urn had **10** *jin* of cooking oil.

Ladle #1 holds **7** *jin*.

Ladle #2 holds **3** *jin*.

Finish

Pour 7 jin into ladle #1 from the urn.

Pour 3 jin into ladle #2 from ladle #1.

Empty ladle #2 into the urn.

Pour another 3 jin into ladle #2 from ladle #1.

Empty ladle #2 into the urn again.

Empty ladle #1 (1 jin) into ladle #2.

Pour 7 jin into ladle #1 from the urn.

Fill up the ladle #2 from ladle #1.

Empty ladle #2 into the urn.

Thus, there are **5** *jin* in ladle #1 and **5** *jin* in the urn.

A poor peasant who lived a simple life in the north of China set out to the market one day with a basket of vegetables, a goat, and a wolf to sell. When they came to the Black Dragon River, there was such a narrow bridge that the peasant could cross it with only one of his commodities at a time. The peasant's dilemma was that he dared not leave the vegetable basket alone with the goat, nor the goat alone with the wolf, lest they be eaten before he returned.

How did the peasant take the vegetables, the goat, and the wolf across the bridge without losing anything for the market?

Start

If the goat were left alone with the vegetables, it would eat them. If the wolf were left alone with the goat, it would eat the goat.

Finish

The peasant first crossed the bridge with the goat, and then he went back for the wolf. But once he had crossed with the wolf, he took the goat back with him over the bridge. Leaving the goat behind, he took the vegetable basket. Only after the vegetable basket was safely across with the wolf did the peasant come back one more time and recross with the goat.

Here is a diagram of the peasant's trips across the bridge:

Peasant crosses with goat ⟶

⟵ Peasant crosses back alone

Peasant crosses with wolf ⟶

⟵ Peasant leads goat back

Peasant carries vegetable ⟶
basket across

⟵ Peasant crosses back alone

Peasant leads goat across ⟶

Peasant, goat, wolf, and vegetable basket are all across the bridge and safe.

One day the Monkey King Sun Wukung, his comrade Zhubajie the Pig, and the monk Tangzen were walking through a village on their way to receive the holy Buddist scripture in India when the Monkey King challenged the Pig to a jumping race. Since they were passing through a villlage, the monk proposed that they race from one end of the village threshing ground, which was 50 yards long, to the other and back again. He gave them a choice. One was allowed to take only **2** jumps of **3** yards each every five seconds, while the other was allowed to take **3** jumps of **2** yards each every 5 seconds. The Pig chose the former, and the Monkey King the latter.

Who made the winning choice?

Start

Although the Monkey King and the Pig were technically supposed to move the same distance of **100** yards and could jump the same distance each five seconds, the Pig was forced, by having to jump **3** yards each time, to jump *past* the edge of the **50**-yard threshing ground.

Finish

The Pig had not realized that 50 is not divisible by 3, and thus he would waste part of 2 jumps. The Monkey King had realized that since 50 was divisible by 2, the number of yards he was allowed to go in each jump, he would not waste any part of any jump.

The Monkey King made the winning choice.

One day an Imperial engineer was ordered by the Emperor to measure the length of a road. However, the engineer had only a single piece of rope and he did not know its exact length. What he was able to learn, however, was that if he stretched this rope out on the road **30** times, it was **2** meters too long. But if he stretched the rope out only **29** times, it was **4** meters short of the end of the road.

Can you figure out the length of both the rope and the road?

Start

30 lengths of rope is 2 meters too long.

29 lengths of rope is 4 meters too short.

Finish

If only one more length of rope were added to 29 lengths, it would be 6 meters long.

$$2 \text{ meters} + 4 \text{ meters} = 6 \text{ meters}$$

Therefore, to calculate the length of the road,

$$(6 \text{ meters} \times 30 \text{ lengths}) - 2\text{meters} = 178 \text{ meters}$$

Thus, the rope is **6** meters long and the road is **178** meters long.

One day while inspecting workers unloading grain from several boats on a rocky river bank, the Bandit King Cao Cao decided to test the intelligence of one of his sons by asking him if he could measure the weight of an elephant that was nearby. Unfortunately, the only scale available was a small one used for weighing sacks of grain.

How did the son satisfy Cao Cao's order, using nothing more than what was around him?

Start

There were several boats on the river.
There were several sacks of grain.
There was also a small scale.

Finish

The Bandit King's son solved the problem by first putting the elephant into a boat and then marking the water line. He then took the elephant out of the boat and loaded the boat with sacks of grain until the boat sank to exactly the same level in the water as when the elephant was on board. Lastly, he directed the workmen to weigh each sack of grain he had put into the boat using the small scale. He then tallied the total weight of all the individual sacks of grain and arrived at the weight of the elephant.